Text copyright ©Anthony Masters 2000
Illustrations copyright © Stephen Player 2000

Published in Great Britain in 2000
by Hodder Wayland, an imprint of
Hodder Children's Books

A catalogue record for this book is available from
British Library.

ISBN: 0 7500 2997 8

Printed in Hong Kong by Wing King Tong

Hodder Children's Books
A division of Hodder Headline Ltd
338 Euston Road, London NW1 3BH

The Shakespeare Collection

MACBETH

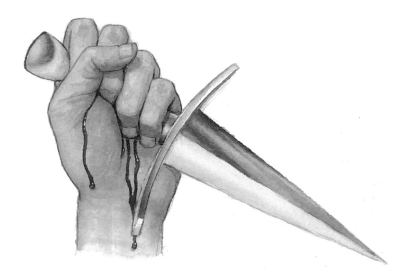

RETOLD BY ANTHONY MASTERS

Illustrated by Stephen Player

HODDER
Wayland

an imprint of Hodder Children's Books

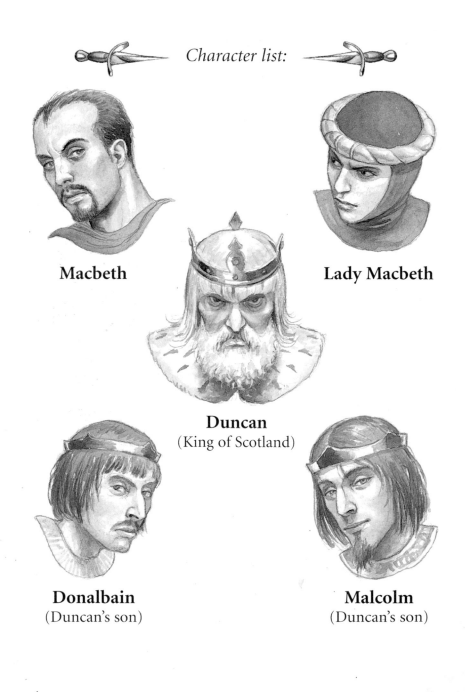

Character list:

Macbeth

Lady Macbeth

Duncan
(King of Scotland)

Donalbain
(Duncan's son)

Malcolm
(Duncan's son)

The three witches

Macduff
(Lord of Fife)

Banquo
(Macbeth's friend)

Ross
(a Scottish noble)

" *I*'ve never seen anything like it!"

Macbeth and his great friend, Banquo, stared at the three witches in horrified amazement. With their withered skins, their wild and straggling hair and their bearded chins, they were a fearful sight.

Macbeth and Banquo, two Scottish generals, were returning home after defeating the invading Norwegians. Their path led across a wind-blasted heath where the three witches often met.

"We can't avoid them," Macbeth told Banquo. "Let's see what they want... Good evening," Macbeth began politely. But each witch put a skinny, stick-like finger to her lips, asking for silence. "What do you want?" he demanded.

The first witch grinned at Macbeth. "Good evening, Lord of Glamis."

He shrugged. "That's the title I'm known by. What do you want?" he repeated.

The second witch grinned even more widely, showing the black stumps of her teeth. "Greetings, Lord of Cawdor."

"I don't have any claim to *that* title." Macbeth was becoming uneasy.

The third witch smiled a cat-like smile. "Welcome, Macbeth, King of Scotland."

Macbeth could never be King of Scotland. His cousin, Duncan, was already king and he had sons who would reign when he died. But Macbeth knew that witches were able to see into the future. Could this be *his* future?

Then one of the witches turned to Banquo and told him a riddle. "You'll be a lesser man than Macbeth. But you'll also be a greater one. Not so happy, but much happier." Banquo would never be King of Scotland, she added, but his sons would be kings instead.

When Macbeth and Banquo tried to ask more questions, the three old hags vanished. The heath was left deserted, with just a whisper of a foul-smelling breeze.

Suddenly two horsemen came thundering across the heath. As the horses sweated to a halt, the two Scottish noblemen, Ross and Angus, jumped down from their saddles.

"We've been sent by the king." Ross was breathless. "He has heard how you defeated the traitor Lord Cawdor after he'd joined the enemy. He has stripped him of his title and is giving it to you, Macbeth. A great honour."

It certainly was. Macbeth was so taken aback that he didn't know what to say. Part of the witches' prophecy had just come true. But what about the rest of it? Could he really be crowned King of Scotland one day? A tiny seed of ambition began to grow inside him.

$\mathcal{M}$acbeth sent a letter to his wife, telling her all that had happened. Lady Macbeth had always been an ambitious woman and when Macbeth arrived home, she suggested a daring plan. They should make the witches' prophecy come true – by murdering the king. King Duncan and his two sons, Donalbain and Malcolm, were all too conveniently visiting the castle that evening.

"It's the chance of a lifetime," insisted Lady Macbeth.

Glamis was a beautiful castle. Swallows had built nests under the buttresses and there was an atmosphere of peace, love and comfort which immediately made King Duncan feel welcome. Tired after his journey, he went to bed early while two of his grooms slept in his state room to guard him.

$\mathcal{M}$acbeth was terrified by the decision that he and Lady Macbeth had made. How could he murder his guest, his king?

He summoned a servant and sent Lady Macbeth an urgent message. "Tell your mistress to ring the bell when my drink is ready," he said. He knew that Lady Macbeth would realize what he really meant: "Ring the bell when it is safe for me to kill the king."

Macbeth then had nothing to do but wait.

Standing alone, time seemed to go so slowly, waiting for the sound of the bell. Staring into the shadows, Macbeth was horrified to see a dagger floating in the air, just in front of him.

"Is this really a dagger I can see before me?" he whispered, trying to grab it. The dagger's handle was pointing towards him but he was clutching at nothing.

Macbeth tried to convince himself that the dagger was just the creation of his guilty mind, but it continued to hover in front of him.

Suddenly its clean blade became stained with blood and Macbeth looked nervously over his shoulder.

"It must be witchcraft," he muttered, sure that his terrible plan had been betrayed. "I beg the very earth itself not to listen to my footsteps," he pleaded. "Don't let the stones cry out and give me away."

Then Macbeth heard the signal. The bell was ringing. It already sounded like King Duncan's death knell.

As Macbeth silently entered the king's bedchamber, Lady Macbeth reached the room next door. Now it was her turn to wait.

"He must be doing it now. I've drugged the grooms' drinks," she muttered, trying to reassure herself. "I've done everything I can."

Then she heard a voice from the king's bedchamber asking, "Who's there?"

Immediately Lady Macbeth was terrified that one of the grooms had woken before her husband had been able to kill the king.

"I laid the daggers ready," she whispered. "He couldn't miss them. If the king hadn't looked so much like my father as he slept I could have killed him myself."

But Macbeth had not failed her.

"I've done it," he said as he joined his wife, and she felt a wave of relief. "It was terrible," Macbeth told her. "One of the grooms cried out: 'Glamis has murdered sleep and therefore Cawdor shall sleep no more. Macbeth shall sleep no more.'"

Lady Macbeth wouldn't allow him to continue. "You had to do it," she insisted. "Soon we'll be King and Queen of Scotland. But why didn't you leave the daggers in the king's chamber? You'll have to take them back."

Macbeth would not go back to the bloody room. So Lady Macbeth sent him to wash Duncan's blood from his hands. Then she took the daggers, moving cautiously through the candle-lit corridors once more.

When she reached the king's bedchamber, Lady Macbeth hurriedly wiped his blood from the blades of the daggers on to the cheeks of the drunken, still sleeping grooms. Now it would look as if *they* were the murderers.

In the morning, Duncan's dead body was discovered.

"This is dreadful!" said Macbeth, openly weeping. "The King's been murdered."

"How dreadful that such a thing should happen in our house," cried Lady Macbeth.

To cover his tracks, Macbeth killed Duncan's two guards – supposedly in fury at their terrible crime. The whole court was in a frenzy of shock.

Realizing that their lives might be in danger, too, Duncan's sons knew that they had to escape.

"I'll go to England," Malcolm told Donalbain. "You travel to Ireland. I fear that none of us are safe here."

$\mathcal{A}$s the witches had promised, Macbeth was soon crowned King of Scotland.

But the witches had also said that Macbeth's children would not inherit the throne. Instead, Banquo's son would be crowned king and Banquo's descendants would rule Scotland.

Macbeth was not prepared to accept this. Now he had tasted power, he was determined to hang on to it. He began to plot against Banquo.

$\mathcal{A}$ great banquet was organized at Macbeth's castle and all the nobility were invited to stay, including Banquo and his son, Fleance.

"I think we'll go out riding this afternoon," Banquo told Macbeth. "But we'll be back in time for the feast."

Macbeth smiled. This gave him just the opportunity he wanted.

As Banquo and Fleance rode back to the castle through the woods in the moonlight, Banquo was uneasy. He kept thinking about the witches' prophecy, some of which had already come true. He and Fleance had heard rumours that Macbeth was involved in Duncan's murder.

Banquo reined in his horse. "What's that?"
he whispered.

"Nothing, father," replied Fleance. "Just an
animal rustling in the bushes."

Suddenly a group of men broke cover.

Although they both put up a fight, in the end Banquo was stabbed to death. Horrified at his father's brutal murder, Fleance made his escape.

Meanwhile, just before the banquet started, Macbeth turned to one of his courtiers and asked, "Where have Banquo and Fleance got to? It's not like them to be late for the feast." But he had already heard the news that Banquo was dead – and that Fleance had escaped.

And as he spoke, Banquo's ghost walked slowly towards him, placing itself on the very chair that he was about to sit on. Macbeth froze, unable to move, staring at his dead friend, appalled at what he had done.

But everyone else only saw Macbeth staring at an empty chair and thought that he had been taken ill.

"What are you doing?" hissed the queen, but Macbeth didn't reply. He was shaking with fear and likely to give them both away.

The queen hurriedly dismissed her guests, making the excuse that her husband was sick.

"You must pull yourself together," she urged Macbeth later.

But Macbeth grew more and more unnerved. He was unable to sleep. He was sure that Banquo's ghost had come for revenge. Fleance's escape also worried him. What's more, an important Scottish noble, Macduff, had failed to attend the banquet. There was a rumour that he had gone to England to raise an army to invade Scotland.

Macbeth decided to visit the witches again.
After all, it was their fault for putting temptation
in his way. Now he wanted to know what his
chances were of surviving as King.

The witches were huddled in a cave near
the windswept heath. They were preparing
a disgusting brew in their magic cauldron
to conjure up spirits to foretell the future.

"You must tell me more of the prophecy," urged Macbeth.

But the witches wouldn't listen, they only stirred their cauldron and chanted:

"Double, double, toil and trouble,
Fire, burn; and cauldron bubble.
Fillet of a fenny snake,
In the cauldron, boil and bake;
Eye of newt, and toe of frog,
Wool of bat—"

"You must answer me!" cried Macbeth in frustration. "Let me see the future."

Without another word the witches called up the spirits. The first was a warrior's head and had a warning for Macbeth: "Beware of the Lord of Fife. Beware Macduff..."

Macbeth nodded. He was already suspicious of Macduff for not attending his banquet. Now he knew that Macduff could not be trusted.

The second spirit rose up in the form of a
bloodied child and told Macbeth to be bold and
determined as 'no man born of woman' would
harm him. Again he felt reassured.

Finally, the third spirit appeared, this time
in the shape of a crowned child with a tree in
his hand.

The child said, "You'll never be defeated until
Birnam Wood starts moving towards Dunsinane
Hill."

Macbeth laughed in relief, knowing that
a forest couldn't possibly move. "But tell me
something else," he asked. "Will Banquo's son
ever become King of Scotland?"

As he spoke, the witches' cauldron sank into the ground and Macbeth heard the sound of strange, haunting music. Then, eight shadowy kings rose up, the last holding a glass which showed a procession of many more ghost-like kings. The ghost of Banquo, covered in blood, stood pointing at them.

With a sinking heart Macbeth realized that all these kings were Banquo's descendants. Whatever was going to happen next?

Only the witches could tell him, but when Macbeth turned to ask them he found that they had vanished.

When Macbeth got back to the castle, one of the nobles brought the news that Macduff had sailed for England. "He's going to join Malcolm's army. They're going to invade Scotland and put Malcolm on the throne."

Calmly and coldly, Macbeth took his terrible revenge. He sent armed men to Macduff's castle, with orders to kill Lady Macduff, her children and even her servants.

The other Scottish lords, horrified at the bloodthirsty murders, immediately joined Malcolm and Macduff's invading army.

Meanwhile, the queen became ill. While Macbeth had become more ruthless, she had become weaker, racked with fear and guilt. She had taken to sleepwalking, roaming the castle at night, convinced she couldn't wash the blood of the murders off her hands. The doctors could do nothing for her.

Macbeth was preparing for Malcolm's invasion when a servant came running to his room.

"The queen, my lord, is dead," he stammered, and Macbeth shivered, knowing he was now alone.

Now Macbeth could only wish for his own death. All too well aware of the approaching army, he decided to shut himself up in his castle.

Almost immediately, however, another messenger, pale and shaking, was shown in to see Macbeth.

"What is it?" demanded the king.

"I was standing guard on the hill when I saw – when I saw – the woods at Birnam begin to move."

Macbeth remembered the witches' prophecy. They had told him that nothing could harm him until Birnam Wood came to Dunsinane Hill. And now the wood was moving!

*I*n truth the wood hadn't moved at all. Malcolm was a skilful general and had told his soldiers to cut down branches of the trees and use them as camouflage as they moved towards the castle.

Yet, still refusing to admit his brief reign as King of Scotland was over, Macbeth took all he had left of his followers and attacked Malcolm's much larger army.

"We'll destroy them," he said. "We've *got* to destroy them."

Macbeth and Macduff came face to face and fought viciously. "You killed my wife and children," Macduff yelled at Macbeth. "You're a tyrant and a murderer."

But Macbeth remembered the words of the spirit that the three witches had summoned up and clung to his one last hope.

"You can't kill me," Macbeth told Macduff. "No one who was born of a woman can hurt me."

But Macduff only smiled triumphantly. "Didn't you know, Macbeth?" he said. "I was taken from my mother's womb before I was due to be born. So I wasn't born naturally at all."

At this, Macbeth felt a surge of panic, but he made one last desperate effort. He threw himself at Macduff and they fought even more viciously than before.

Then Macduff drew on his last ounce of strength, swung his sword and Macbeth's head rolled on to the ground, coming to rest at his feet.

Macduff bent down and picked up the severed head and made a present of it to the lawful king, Malcolm.

With Macbeth dead, the nobles all hailed Malcolm as their rightful king. A new time of peace was dawning in Scotland.

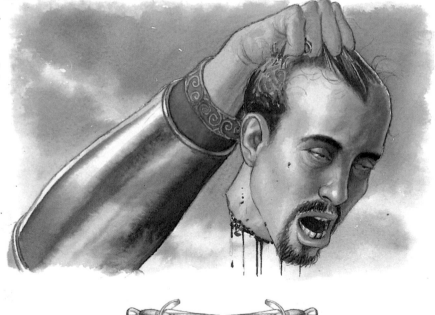

The Shakespeare Collection

Look out for these other titles in the Shakespeare Collection:

A Midsummer Night's Dream Retold by Clare Bevan
What happens when the fairy world and the mortal world collide? Disaster! Demetrius is in love with Hermia, who is in love with Lysander, who is in love with Helena, who is in love with Demetrius! Will they ever sort out this mess, or do they need a little help from the fairies?

Much Ado About Nothing Retold by Jan Dean
Beatrice and Benedick swear they hate each other, Claudio and Hero swear they love each other. Will Claudio and Hero persuade Beatrice and Benedick that love and marriage are good things?

Romeo and Juliet Retold by Rebecca Lisle
The Capulets and Montagues have always hated each other, so when Romeo falls in love with his enemy's daughter, they must keep their love a secret. If they are discovered it could mean war between the two families...

You can buy all these books from your local bookseller, or order them direct from the publisher. For more information about The Shakespeare Collection, write to: *The Sales Department, Hodder Children's Books, a division of Hodder Headline Limited, 338 Euston Road, London NW1 3BH.*

TGIHP

Thank God I Have Problems

MATHEW VERGHESE

Tate Publishing & Enterprises

Published by Tate Publishing & Enterprises, LLC
127 E. Trade Center Terrace | Mustang, Oklahoma 73064 USA
1.888.361.9473 | www.tatepublishing.com

Tate Publishing is committed to excellence in the publishing industry. The company reflects the philosophy established by the founders, based on Psalm 68:11,
"The Lord gave the word and great was the company of those who published it."

Published in the United States of America

ISBN: 978-1-60799-257-8
Self-Help / Motivational & Inspirational
09.07.27

TOC

ACKNOWLEDGEMENTS

I would not have been able to have any of these experiences without the support and encouragement of my wife, Sheila, and my children, Luke, Priya and Simon. Their unconditional love has enabled me to move along in life. To my parents for directing me to the correct direction in my life and to my brother and sister who have always been with me in the growing stages of my life.

I owe a lot to my colleagues and friends at various firms and locations for trusting me and listening to me for advice and help. You have been there for me and have been as extended family all these years. I have always considered you and friends and as family and always will.

I could not have managed with all the situations in life without the guidance and providence of my Jesus. The comforting words in the Bible like—

"Don't be afraid, just believe" Mark 5:36 (NIV)

"Without *me*, you can do nothing" John 15:5 (NKJV)

"Give thanks in *all* circumstances" 1 Thes 5: 18 (NIV)

"In his heart a man plans his course, but the LORD determines his steps" Proverbs 16:9 (NIV)

—have been my cornerstone and nourishment. Life is useless unless we have a commitment to God Almighty.

The fullness of life with a combination of all these make life worth living.

—Mathew

INTRODUCTION

Normal business books are written by well-known 'Wall Street' names, folks that have been successful and have made tremendous amounts of money and a name in the business world, or have recognizable pictures. Sure I know him or her, but who is this person?

Sorry, I have none of this.

I am still a work-in-progress.

What I offer is a simple, down-to-earth experience, from the ground up. The good thing with our world is that opportunities are tremendous and open for all. Just a handful of individuals take the dive and venture into the fun world of the unknown—troubles, ups and downs, frustrations and depressions, sleepless nights. But, it comes with a bundle of joy, accomplishment and life experience that one cannot explain. Management schools only point you to opportunities; individuals need to make the move into what they like, and get into the world of adventure.

I believe that God has a good plan and purpose for all. In critical phases of life or during crossroads, He will guide us through the correct path. It's almost like the GPS we have in cars. If we ever take a wrong exit or path, the GPS will redirect you to the right track again. The point is that we *do* take wrong exits and paths all the time. I know that GPS—*G*od *P*rovides for us *S*inners, is what we should depend on. Big name and fame are not for all. Living a purposeful life with passion is what we should achieve, all the rest will follow.

While I have tried to run through my business life in a sweeping chapter, the focus is on pointing out some of the important elements that I feel are placed in the back burner of companies. We need to take them out, dust them, polish them, and make them stand out firm as our important areas to concentrate.

My hope is the readers will be benefited by this book and be encouraged that they are not unique to problems in business or this life as such. Problems happen to a lot of companies and to lot of people, in-fact to all.

Let us read other's experiences to better our business, our life, and make our world better.

—Mathew

MY WORLD

One of the first bits of advice that I ever got before starting off as an entrepreneur was from a good lawyer friend of mine. He said, "If anything can go wrong in business, it will." If it were not for the encouragement of my wife, Sheila, I would have started to look for another job. But, by her great *success* card and by the Grace of God, I did venture in the unknown world of *business*.

Although I did have a formal education in economics, accounting, and management, the real world of business really was unexpected and I must admit exciting. Here is my story...the business story.

It is the normal immigrants story—two suitcases and $20 in the pocket, converted from hard-earned savings from working in India, and the only money left over from paying for the one-way airfare. The plane landed in New York's JFK. One of my bags was totally damaged, but a good bag handler had taped the bag with some airline duct tape. Actually only half the bag remained. Still, I was excited to come to the country and meet my family. My mother had stayed on in the US with my sister and family to make sure that I was in the country safely and as per the sponsor rules. My sister, a doctor, and her great husband, who is in the insurance business, had this big house in northwest New York. They worked in Manhattan and left early in the morning and came back late at night. It took me a few days to clear the jet lag and make that Manhattan trip. In the meantime, I unknowingly saw a good part of the day's soaps on TV, which drove me insane, but at that time, I was patient enough to bear it out. Still excited about job prospects, the two feet of snow and borrowed shoes and overcoats did not bother me much.

My first solo venture into this new world alone was on a public bus to the local mall and town area. The walk to the bus stop was long and walking in so much snow was not part of my past experience. The bus stopped, to my surprise, very empty. The almost honor system bus fare of 35 cents, to be dropped into a coin slot, was closely monitored by the driver. I walked almost aimlessly at my destination to look for a job. After the normal window shopping, I did notice an office that offered job placements. I fearlessly walked in and asked to see the manager who could get me a job. I was directed to fill in a long form with all my personal details. It did not take me long, being a fast writer. I was then called into the office and the manger interviewed me. He let me speak for a while and then quickly cut me off saying that although my education and qualifications were great, I had no US experience, and therefore, he flat out could not help me. Very curt and direct! Since I was not used to this kind of presentation, it pulled me down. That was when, I know, the first thoughts to repack and go back to India crept into my mind.

The maiden trip to Manhattan was exciting; big buildings, busy streets, important people, good-looking suits and clothes. Everyone walked fast on the roads; they seem to be doing very important things, except me. I just hung around, walked the streets, entered into the library, and tried to read and look intellectual. Lots of 'hi's'. No job. No that was not true, I had a few job offers, a cargo loader in a large retail store, maybe an underwriter, an unpaid IT person for a placement firm in mid-town Manhattan. He did offer his old car to me for use and maybe lunch once a while. Somehow I had the courage to refuse this job as well. All these were a blow to my American dream. The bubble was nearly blown. To me, the 10 days of wandering did not do much for my self-esteem. I was down to the last straw after this. My mother, sister, and brother-in-law kept encouraging me to wait and keep trying. I was almost ready to pack up and return to India. At least I had a job there and had some assistance in work with a "manager" title.

Almost on a last pitch, I then picked up the phone and started making some calls. Networking they call it. All my management school mates and friends that I knew with phone numbers were called and asked if they knew of any positions for me. It worked! A classmate who was working in Atlanta, made the introductions to a Detroit-based IT firm. After two days of interviews, I was offered the positions of an HR manager that I gladly took. I worked diligently for five years. While expectations are different, I took pride in being honest at work and gave my best. Granted, I did not reach to the caliber of others. But, I had this dream of doing my own business. As time moved on, I did make a break to start my own business.

I really did not have any sales, marketing, or finance experience. But I prayed for strength from God Almighty, and He gave me the power to reach out and venture into this unknown world. Again,

I picked up the phone and started talking to folks that I know and some I did not know, and I had lots of encouraging feedback that started to build my confidence.

One of the first businesses that I closed was a $3000 fee for finding a perfect candidate for a Pittsburgh firm. I worked with someone on this with an understanding that I would get half of this amount. The terms were that I would get this amount 90 days after this person was on the project. I waited patiently for this 90-day term and prepared (for the first time) an invoice for $1500. I did make several calls and was promised payment. I waited and waited. Now that was in the year 1994 and I am yet to be paid. They call it bad debt, but a big red flag on the firm that left me without payment. Never to work with them again! I never had this kind of experience before. That company did call me several years later for some help, and needless to say, I just hung up. That was my first deal, or a theoretical deal.

The ups and downs in business have been evident after that. Good people come in and join with promises to stay for a long time, but only a few actually stay and are faithful. Some join with smooth conversations of giving you the world, nothing happens and they turn against you, with their friends. They stop talking and in the end you are the bad guy. I take it all in. Patience, is always a virtue, I was told. Never fight back, listen and be understanding. My poor wife gets the raw brunt of all this. Although I share only the highlights of the business with her, that is a lot for her to take. And yes, there is no clear cut answer for anything. All in good time, and I believe this.

The toughest part in business is letting go of anyone. Personally, this is an emotional drain on me. I take a lot of pride in people and give them time to make themselves productive at work. I hold on to them to the point of creating a large overhead, but being fair goes beyond overhead expenses. The intentions are to pay for the fair work. If some-one who is productive leaves, at least in my eyes, it takes me weeks to recover. Sometimes I just shut my office door and do not have the strength to face the rest of the world. I am still working on this. This is the emotional part that is trying.

One simple business rule is to return phone calls to all employees and of course customers. I am yet to understand why this cannot be the policy for all. Maybe they are too busy. When I started the business, there was no Internet, and no cell phone for emails. I thought life would be faster and easier with all these wonderful tools and gadgets. (Looks as if we take more work home and more problems from work.) Sure we can work from home etc, etc, but family time is smaller and smaller.

Over the business growth, the need to give up micro-management and dependence on others grew. I had to pass on work to others and let them take ownership of their territory. Talking to them over lunch and some regulated business meetings and timings works well with all. Everybody loves being given charge of their area. Their commitment, leadership, and initiative will blossom from this independence. They will take ownership. Sure interpersonal issues always crop up, but the role of the leader is to just encourage and give warm words of comfort and uplifting emails. They, just like you, love to get a pat on the back. I love to get a good remark in the email.

Clearly, we can handle only what we can and can grow to a certain comfort level that we can. Basically, we all have limits in our capabilities, while we may not openly admit it. Some of us, like me, have sleepless nights thinking of options and want to bounce ideas off key team members before we launch a new area or project.

Now, over the years, I have met, read and seen a number of firms grow from ground up, some faster than others. But there seems to be something missing in most of them. I call it the three missing departments in business. I have made an attempt to spell these out with detail in the next chapters.

2

CASH FLOW MANAGEMENT (CFM)

Cash Flow Management, CFM, is one of the subjects that needs to be taught more aggressively in management schools. A business needs cash flow management (CFM) to run properly.

Sometimes when customers are slow to pay, we may suggest that they need a lot of approvals and checks and balances. True in most cases, but often this is also on account of them managing their cash or CFM. Maybe they are not paid by *their* customers on time. We may need to understand where we stand in the food chain and calculate when we can best be paid for our services. If we deal with credit cards or only up-front payment, then we can skip this chapter; however, there could be services we use that require us to understand this side of the business well.

I therefore suggest the following course material for this (CFM) management class:

1. How to manage our customers:
    Customers are the most important part of any business. Customers are always right. Customers bring in the money. All true, but if they do not pay in time, we quickly do not want them as customers.

    Personally, I have had several experiences with non-paying customers. We get a customer after a lot of hard work—real hard work, sometimes taking them out for lunches and events, giving some goodies at times too. Finally they give us a work to do. We do our best, put in extra time and manpower to get the work done, and when we deliver, some of them come up with some unreasonable excuse for not paying.

Ever been through that?

Really frustrating! Another common path that bigger companies take is that they do not have the department head approval, or the business head is traveling and will be back in 10–15 days. That person's approval is necessary to get this passed on to accounting. Delays in accounting are also to be expected. Sometimes, it gets more creative. Only a part payment is made and we would spend months to reconcile this matter. It really hits the bottom then. Of course there is the usual voicemail fronts that we all face. Voice mails are returned conveniently after working hours when surely the business is closed for the day. Surely customers are in important meetings the whole day, so important that they cannot call back in a while.

I think this course should list out all different strategies to get to the right person at the right day and time to collect, how to talk, whom to talk to, what times work best, and how to get from plan A to plan B. What strategies we need to take to ensure that in spite of this eventuality, we actually make out, in terms of our desired margins. When to start charging interest, how often should we call the person, what levels we need to take this to.

2. How to manage our vendors:

Now we are at the other side of the table. They will be making calls to you. How do we manage them?

The important factor here is to manage expectations. If we have this straight and a history of payments, the calls will be less. Of course, having a signed agreement is important, however as we know the intent of the agreement is more important than the agreement itself. Any lawyer will tell you that.

There are the critical vendors that you have to pay to run the business, of course. Phone, Internet providers, utilities, and computers are critical to get the work going. Never delay these at any cost. The rest are more agreeable to terms and longer payment cycle.

3. How to manage our employee expenses:

The simple rule is employees are golden. As an employer we always need to pay salaries on time, unless you build an expectation that salary could be late, due to an explained reason. Expenses need to be managed. This could be all over the place. For example, if we have an unlimited relocation policy, then I have seen employees going up to $5000 and above for a single person relocation. If we in turn tell them that the total relocation cost policy of the company is $1500, which is an allowance, I have seen them working with this amount and even keeping some in the bank. It is important to keep such controls for all. Staged approval is also necessary. Scheduling reimbursement payment helps some too. Commissions can be paid after the customer pays us. These are some of the tips to manage cash internally with employees.

4. Management tool to cash management:

Admittedly, most firms do not have extensive financial software to manage their books. While these are expensive and need costly manpower to manage, the good old excel works well for all. There are smaller and cheaper software programs out there that I recommend to be used, but simple month-by-month comparisons of income and expenses need to be done on a timely basis, every month, and discussed with the team. They need to know what their performance is against targets.

5. How to make others pay:

I have seen many first use the sub-contractor approach and more recently the outsourcing model. What happens in this outsourcing model is that work is paid for based on the output without the HR (human resources) issues that an employer has to face. This is a great tool to shift the HR responsibility to others and focus on taking care of the customers needs. But more importantly the best tool for cash management. Let others invest in the capital expenses, HR, office space, retention, attrition, administration, sexual harassment matters. We just pay for the good work, not the bad work done. In this scenario, as an employer we can demand higher standards from our vendors, not involved in local issues and conditions, we only focus on the output and its quality.

The offshore model of today is even a better invention. We get all of the above and super cost savings also. Granted, some specialized firms call for a niche experience; however, to bring them up to the standards, the offshore company most of the time eats the training cost and then is paid the full agreed price once the performance is reached. Also, there is a time lag in billing and being paid. Then there are these large contracts giving control of the intellectual property rights that keep all this with the control of the owners. The idea is not a negative spin—just a great cash management idea of our times.

6. Customer history and credit:

Every person in business has dealt with a customer that just does not want to pay. Comments like, "the project is not what the customer wants," or "missed the deadline by two days," etc. so they cannot pay, do not have any merit. These complaints, in most cases, are after constant monitoring of the project and emails or weekly calls. Sometimes they wanted to see this to show their customers to get a bigger project for themselves. I have seen this more often for projects done offshore. I have personally faced situation like "we can only pay after we get the source code of the software." I am sure some of you have gone through all this also at some point of the offshore management.

Clearly, in these cases, we need to ask for upfront payment along with set payment terms. While most projects are structured this way, normally there is increasing emphasis on the back-end payment. Keep a close watch on this. Sometimes just to open doors, we may fall into this trap of being paid after the work is done, especially for small projects.

7. What is one cash payment that we should never miss:

Again, never miss paying salary for employees. If by any chance salary payment will be late, build that expectation upfront. Payroll is critical to keep employees to keep the business going. There is no business without employees who get the customers and keep them happy. If you have ever dealt with a bank line of credit and have almost reached the credit limit, then you know that when it's payroll going through this credit line, banks let it go through, even if it has passed some credit limit. Banks know that this is critical for running the business.

CFM is critical for running any business and of course personal family lives too.

3

TWO STEPS AHEAD TEAM (TSAT)

True thinking out of the box is what would make us different in the very competitive world. But do we think ahead? My proposal is to have a "Two Steps Ahead Team" or TSAT. This team just works and thinks above the curve. They would analyze all current issues and how each issue could impact the company if we choose this new project or the other. What is not emphasized is the impact of a decision on the company based on trends and the future. What is our backup of the backup plan? How much time do we spend on these items?

Each department is broken down into different functions, then, those different functions into different roles and responsibilities. Try to document issues in each of these headings. Let the list roll. The important factor is to list issues.

I think a more creative approach is a mandatory report by every employee in the company before they leave for the day, to document all issues they had that day and how it was taken care of. Within months, if not days, all the possible issues in the company can be listed down. These need to be categorized and presented to the "Two Steps Ahead Team." They would then have solutions options listed out. So, if a new employee joins the company, they would know as part of the orientation, all the problems that they could face while working for the company and possible solutions. Surely they can suggest alternative solutions to the problem, but they already have working solutions.

What happens is that we waste a lot of time learning on the job rather than doing the job. We need, in this process, to have solutions to issues and focus on the job, therefore productivity increases.

Normally I would give a new employee about 3–6 months to be productive. Say a good salary for a person is averaged at $40,000 a year, that is $3333.33 a month plus 30% overhead cost would bring the cost per month to $4333.33 a month. A three-month cost would be $12,999.99 and a six months cost would be $25,999.99. Lets say there are ten new employees for a mid size firm; the total relatively slow months would cost the company a whopping $259,999.99 for the six months. That is a lot of money spent for just experimenting . Clearly there are some brighter ones that are hired. But even a $200,000 investment is a costly expense for any company, and that is assuming the person staying on in the company for that long.

The costliest resource is manpower and there is a tremendous need to get this working right from day one. We need to put serious thought how to mange this correctly and quickly. Really think about it. How many of us really do this? Do we take this seriously and come up with an action plan for this expense?

That is why the *TSAT* is key for any industry.

Lets see, in my companies, I can bet you if I actually counted all the problems that I had, it could not be more than actually 50–60 per company. Then there is the timing, personality issues, location, business cycle, division, etc. that have to be addressed, but surely, it can be documented. Why don't we do this? We just want to give the employees freedom to do their thing. While this might work for a few employees with enough and more drive, the majority of them need direction.

I guess we have to define what a problem is first. Let me try.

A problem occurs when I do not know what to do at that point of time, while working in my company (or at this point in my life).

Maybe I have simplified this too much. Just think about it for a moment. That's it! The question is what do I do? Sure we can ask others and get the answers, get their opinions, but in most managed firms, the team is limited and we have to go to the boss, who is hardly around and is busy in the office doing other work. So, let's go to this problem, given the situation, here are what others did with the similar problem. Okay, now we have some options to pick from and meaningful options with real world solutions.

No, no, this is not just theory. Just think about it slowly ... it's possible.

4

CRISIS TEAM (CT)

Most of management time is taken to "put out the fire" and not to open more doors for business. Every day, morning to evening, sometime through the night, if we have international locations, we face issues that need to be addressed ASAP. My suggestion is to have a Crisis Team (CT) that does this all the time. These are trained experts that have a book, manual, or system that literally has all issues that my business could ever have and implement the solution based on past success stories. True, situations may be different, but I have seen that more of the matters are similar in nature and can be documented. Do we have a function like CT that has built this over the years, months, or even weeks to offer a solution?

While the government may have such CTs in place for the state and Federal level, do we really have this for a company? Is it cost effective? Will it help?

All good questions! When we are in the middle of such a crisis, if we do not have a plan in place, we tend to use valuable client facing time with routine management work that could be dealt by others.

This is based on historic facts and numbers. Industry wise, information is different. If information is confidential of some sort, then the company internally must generate this information and have consultants that just do this.

In business we know there are two types of issues that may come up. One normal business matters like employee attrition and the likes. However in a training company the critical employees are the trainers and if there is a shortage of these, it would directly affect the performance of this firm's ability to provide training services. The normal business matters already have a team in place to handle like in this case of attrition; it's the Human Resource department. But how do we handle problems like having two of the three trainers having stomach flu at the same time? How do we handle a group of students who are waiting and paid for scheduled classes? First, we do not know how long the illness may last. Secondly, we have a group of real unhappy students who have schedules and deadlines. While there may be a number of quick fix solutions for this kind of situations, the critical issue is that we are prepared for such an eventuality and how quickly we respond to such a situation.

Wow, lets look at the options that we might have here:

1. Tie up with close related firms that may offer a quick overlap training.

2. Possibly resort to a quick internet method of training.

3. Take them forward a few steps to another group to see if they might fit in to keep them working.

The important thing is to have options and have the options ready for us at short notice, in fact, very short notice.

Recently I bought a new computer. Based on prior experience, I went all out to get a good email system using an external server option to retrieve my email, contacts, and calendar options. And then what else could go wrong? As you can expect, I did write a good part of this book on the machine and was confident that nothing would happen. You guessed right, the system crashed. I felt devastated! All the hard work was simply gone. Maybe you have gone through this many a time, final paper for school, presentation to a customer, important meeting notes at office, business talk points after long hours of work—hard work and no backup. It turned out that I did take a long extended warranty of the computer, which saved paying additional costs and the hard drive being revived. The in-between time was certainly uncertain and caused some unnecessary concern. Why do we go through this? I know some of you have gone through this.

We all use our computers often and are dependent on this for work, home, and for all other activities.

Why do we repeat this over and over again in our lives? Maybe we think that things cannot happen again or things cannot happen to me. Sure I have heard others telling me about it, read about it, but why *does* it happen to me?

Good question, but the answer is that it happens to all at some time of the life cycle.

While this is a personal disaster when it happens to one person, just think for a moment if it happens to a company. For example, a virus can be devastating in a firm that hires employees, and if they cannot access computer, Internet, or email, for that matter. Things will come to a grinding halt and the make-up time is long drawn.

Have the CT take over and remedy the problem ASAP. A good back-up system and keeping files critical to the firm's operations located a central server, maybe in another location, where employees can get to work on projects. Surely some thinking needs to go into this and how it will work.

Situations and circumstances are different. It may look difficult from an outside perspective, but an internal person can easily identify this and provide the information to the CT well in advance.

Even in our personal lives, lots of issues that come up can be made easier if there is CT in place. How about the time when the front door locks on you by mistake or a wind that blows the door shut? Gone through that? Only a few think of keeping a spare key with a friend or under a safe spot. We can come up with many CT solutions to our life's problems. Do we invest some time into this?

It sure would make our life easier!

5

MOVING FORWARD

Now listen to me. There are only a bunch of issues in this world. We are all in this world to live and to achieve the best purpose that God planned for us. The world would be such a better place if we have a master file of these issues documented and available for a nominal fee. True industry wise issues, location wise issues, country wise issues, etc, do play a key role in the outcome, but would not the world be a better place if we have most of the issues listed for our generation to see? Do we really have to research each time to get to what we want? We would do just the best for our children and the future if these are recorded and made available. Any confidential, direct business matter could be kept in a deposit for an agreed time period, say seven years and then made available.

Maybe we should also keep life's, marriage, growing up issues, etc., so that we have a quick reference to these matters. I really do not want to know what it all means, I just want a good, viable way out of this mess that has come my way. We need to stop and think that any issues that we face are not unique to us or specially designed for 'me'. This has been around for a while and probably will be there till the end of times.

Any takers?

We have tried to list out all the problems in the world in an open website called www.tgihp. com (Thank God I have problems). The attempt is to have folks list their issues and have others fill in for them the different solutions to issues in life. There could be your solution to this problem both in the business and personal world. Why do we go through with this when we know that others have great solutions to issues and they have worked it out well?

There is a sense of comfort to know that others have gone through similar issues in their life. Nothing is brand new.

So keep smiling and go to www.tgihp.com.

This story goes on.

God Bless you.